50 THINGS
BOO...
REVIEWS FROM READERS

I recently downloaded a couple of books from this series to read over the weekend thinking I would read just one or two. However, I so loved the books that I read all the six books I had downloaded in one go and ended up downloading a few more today. Written by different authors, the books offer practical advice on how you can perform or achieve certain goals in life, which in this case is how to have a better life.

The information is simple to digest and learn from, and is incredibly useful. There are also resources listed at the end of the book that you can use to get more information.

50 Things To Know To Have A Better Life: Self-Improvement Made Easy!

Author Dannii Cohen

This book is very helpful and provides simple tips on how to improve your everyday life. I found it to be useful in improving my overall attitude.

50 Things to Know For Your Mindfulness & Meditation Journey
Author Nina Edmondso

Quick read with 50 short and easy tips for what to think about before starting to homeschool.

50 Things to Know About Getting Started with Homeschool by Author Amanda Walton

I really enjoyed the voice of the narrator, she speaks in a soothing tone. The book is a really great reminder of things we might have known we could do during stressful times, but forgot over the years.

Author Harmony Hawaii

There is so much waste in our society today. Everyone should be forced to read this book. I know I am passing it on to my family.

50 Things to Know to Downsize Your Life: How To Downsize, Organize, And Get Back to Basics

Author Lisa Rusczyk Ed. D.

Great book to get you motivated and understand why you may be losing motivation. Great for that person who wants to start getting healthy, or just for you when you need motivation while having an established workout routine.

50 Things To Know To Stick With A Workout: Motivational Tips To Start The New You Today

Author Sarah Hughes

50 THINGS TO KNOW ABOUT THE CELTA COURSE

Acing Your ESL Certification Course

Catherine Camilleri

50 Things to Know About The CELTA Course Copyright © 2021 by CZYK Publishing LLC.
All Rights Reserved.

All rights reserved. No part of this book may be reproduced in any form or by any electronic or mechanical means including information storage and retrieval systems, without permission in writing from the author. The only exception is by a reviewer, who may quote short excerpts in a review.

The statements in this book are of the authors and may not be the views of CZYK Publishing or 50 Things to Know.

Cover designed by: Ivana Stamenkovic
Cover Image: https://pixabay.com/photos/girl-english-dictionary-read-2771936/

CZYK Publishing Since 2011.
CZYKPublishing.com
50 Things to Know

Lock Haven, PA
All rights reserved.

ISBN: 9798848959987

50 THINGS TO KNOW ABOUT THE CELTA COURSE

BOOK DESCRIPTION

Are you interested in teaching English as a Second Language? Are you passionate about meeting people from around the world? Are you ready for a challenge? If you answered yes to any of these questions, then this book is for you!

"50 Things to Know about the CELTA Course" by author Catherine Camilleri offers a personal approach to mastering this highly intensive, Cambridge University course. Most books on CELTA tell you the logistics of the course. Although there is nothing wrong with that, this book gives you an in-depth and personal look inside the classroom. Based on knowledge from the world's leading experts, more and more teachers are choosing to take the CELTA to reach new opportunities in the ESL field.

In these pages you will discover how to plan your lessons, the different skills you'll learn, and an look inside the fundamentals of CELTA. This book will help you prepare for the CELTA and get to know some of the things you will encounter during the course.

By the time you finish this book, you will know how to navigate the ins and outs of the course and save yourself time and energy by answering your questions about the adventure you are about to embark on. So, grab YOUR copy today. You will be glad you did.

TABLE OF CONTENTS

50 Things to Know
Book Series
Reviews from Readers
BOOK DESCRIPTION
TABLE OF CONTENTS
DEDICATION
ABOUT THE AUTHOR
INTRODUCTION
1. Getting into the CELTA Course.
2. What You Need to Pass
3. Full Time vs. Part Time
4. Taking the CELTA While Working
5. Expenses
6. Choosing Where to Take Your Course
7. Location is Key
8. CELTA and COVID-19
9. Personal Life on Pause
10. Forget About that diet
11. Pre-Tasks
12. Preparing for the Course
13. Necessary Tech
14. The Night Before
15. First Day Jitters
16. Working Together: Meet Your Peers

17. Meet Your Instructors
18. Trusting Your Instructors
19. Meet Your Students
20. Breaking the Ice
21. Culture Shock
22. Motives for Learning
23. Let the Students be the Teachers
24. The Do's and Do Not's of Teaching
25. Not the Worst Teacher in the World
26. Feedback
27. TP (Teaching Practice) Prep
28. Monitoring Students during Observation
29. Monitoring Students During your Lessons
30. Lesson Types
31. Lesson Planning
32. Pre-Teach
33. Target Language
34. Authentic Material
35. Phonics
36. Grammar Analysis
37. What is TTT
38. What is PPP
39. What is MFP
40. What are CCQs
41. What are ICQs
42. Time Management: In the Classroom

43. 1st Assignment: Focus on the Learner
44. 2nd Assignment: Language Related Task
45. 3rd Assignment: Language Skills Task
46. 4th Assignment: Lessons from the Classroom
47. Balancing Under Pressure
48. Time Management: At Home
49. Now You Have Your CELTA, What Next?
50. Other Courses

Other Helpful Resources:

50 Things to Know

DEDICATION

I would like to dedicate this book to my CELTA instructors, Brigid and Angie, whose patience and dedication helped me master this course. I would also like to dedicate this to the other teachers who went on this journey with me; without your help and guidance, I would not be the teacher I am today. A big thanks to IELS Malta and Cambridge University for allowing us to continue the course even as COVID-19 struck, and a shout-out to the students, who acted as our guinea pigs and helped us practice our teaching.

ABOUT THE AUTHOR

: Catherine Camilleri is a Cambridge certified ESL teacher, freelance writer, editor, and poet. She graduated from State University of New York at Purchase College with degrees in Creative Writing and Literature and was awarded the Ginny Wray Senior Prize in Poetry. A native New Yorker who currently lives in Malta, Catherine spends her time teaching students from around the world, and writing stories and poems about her native land, fantasy worlds, and Greek myths. She is an active member of LGBTQI+Gozo and Malta Arch, an organization aimed to uphold Maltese ecology and heritage. She can be reached for lessons, writing, and editing at cat.camilleri@outlook.com

INTRODUCTION

"Teaching is like trying to hold 35 corks underwater at once."

– Mark Twain

Teaching has always been on the forefront of my mind when I thought about the career I wanted to pursue. I have always loved reading and writing and found myself building lesson plans while in school. During particularly boring classes, I would imagine how I would teach the class and even thought about topics that I would want to teach, like Personification in Literary Philosophy, Women Characters who Shape our Adolescence and Greek Mythology's Relevance in Modern Literature. I knew that teaching was the ultimate goal and once I finished university, I was ready to take that step to become an English teacher.

I decided to move to Malta, mainly to maintain my independence after college, but also to experience my ancestral land and live in Europe. Before the big move across the Atlantic, I discovered

CELTA; it seemed like an amazing opportunity and a challenge to myself, to test my skills and gain firsthand experience. Armed with grand plans, I flew across the pond and got ready to embark on this new journey. However, the best laid plans of mice and men often go awry— COVID-19 struck a week into my CELTA course and the world began its descent into isolation, masks, PPE, and quarantines.

But there was a silver-lining: the CELTA course would not be canceled. Instead, the normally three-week program would be extended, and everything shifted to online. I quickly learned how to teach via Zoom, I adopted a cat, moved next to my grandparents, and completed the course two months later. I met some amazing teachers and wonderful instructors, and, armed with my CELTA certification, began finding students of my own. I now teach students of all ages from around the world, without leaving my apartment and often still in my pajama pants.

Taking this course taught me how to be a stronger, smarter, more compassionate teacher and opened the door to lifelong opportunities. The beauty about CELTA is that you can teach anywhere in the world or from the comfort of your own home, meeting people from around the globe and sharing your knowledge to help others reach their full potential. There is nothing more fulfilling then walking away from a lesson knowing that you left a lasting impression on a student.

Teachers are the unsung heroes in our lives, who can help us in the simplest of ways on our journey through this crazy thing we call our existence. They help us realize our goals and push us to be the best we can be. Despite the ups and downs, teachers remain a vital part of our experiences and can change the course of our lives in the most meaningful ways.

1. GETTING INTO THE CELTA COURSE.

There are two components to getting into the CELTA course, besides your initial application: the interview and the test. Once you have decided where you want to take the course, you will be asked to go in and take a brief test regarding grammar, writing and comprehension. I was a nervous wreck when taking my initial test. Even though I had studied up the weeks before, I remember staring at the paper in front of my, thinking I was a fool. But I did my best, and once the interview came around, the nervousness was gone. During the interview, you will review your answers with the interviewer, who will discuss what you need to work on prior to the course. You will talk about why you want to take the course, and why you are passionate about teaching. The interviewer will tell you all that will be expected of you in the coming weeks, so you have a clear idea about what you need to do to prepare. Have a few questions prepared to ask the interviewer, either about the logistics of the course or personal queries about your own expectations. The interviewer will usually tell you then and there if you can participate in the course or an email will be sent to you, in addition to pertinent information. In my case, the instructor told me immediately that I was granted a spot in the course and the next part of the CELTA journey begun.

2. WHAT YOU NEED TO PASS

Let us break down what exactly you need to pass the CELTA. First and foremost, you must be present for all teaching practices and tutorials. CELTA is extremely strict about attendance and will only excuse an absence for an absolute emergency. Even then, teaching practice and tutorials that were missed must be made up, so the is little wiggle room when it comes to attendance. Second, you need to complete 6 hours of observation of an experienced classroom teacher, which will take place during your tutorials. You also need to complete 8 assessed teaching practice lessons, each 45 minutes long. Lastly, a pass on 3 out of 4 detailed assignments. The good thing about these assignments is that you have a chance to revise your assignment after feedback, something every CELTA student will take advantage of. At the end of the course, you will be given either a Pass, Pass B, Pass A or Fail. Pass A and Pass B are exceedingly difficult scores to get and are rarely granted. Most successful teachers receive a Pass— so do not compare your grade with other teachers who may have more experience or time in the classroom.

3. FULL TIME VS. PART TIME

After careful deliberation, I decided to take the full time CELTA course. This is completed in three weeks and crams months' worth of study and teaching practice into a short time. While daunting, I ultimately decided that three weeks would fly by (see CELTA and COVID). If the intensive, full-time course seems too stressful, never fear; the part-time course is a nice medium, with classes held three times a week instead of each day. The course might take longer, but there is greater room for error. Initially, I was planning on taking the part-time course and commute throughout the week, but the ESL school offered hotel accommodations nearby, which cut down my expected travel time exponentially. There are numerous factors to consider when choosing between full and part time, but ultimately, you must choose what will work best for you. If you thrive under pressure and are the type of person who relishes a challenge, then the full-time course is for you. If you prefer a little more breathing room and a more relaxed environment, then part-time is the road to take.

4. TAKING THE CELTA WHILE WORKING

If you currently have a job and are considering the CELTA, be sure to alert your supervisors that you will be unavailable for the duration of the course. Even if you decide on the part-time course, you will not have the time or energy to commit to your job. During my CELTA, one of my peers learned this the hard way. He was unable to finish the course because of the mounting pressures from his employer; granted, because of COVID, our course was greatly extended, and my colleague had already taken time from work, but could not afford to take more time off. Many of my other trainers were in similar situations and were able to finagle extra time away from work. If you are already a teaching in a school, plan your course around summer breaks and extended vacations. Be prepared to put your job on hold and take the necessary time off to focus solely on the course. For those already in the teaching field and work for a school, your superiors might be more willing to give you time off to take the course, they may even sponsor you if they feel certain you will pass.

5. EXPENSES

When choosing what course is right for you, expense needs to be considered. The CELTA is an expensive course, at around $3000 for the course itself, including registration and deposits. The CELTA is definitely an investment, but the pros outweigh the cons— the CELTA allows you to teach anywhere in the world and CELTA teachers can ask for higher pay. The CELTA never expires, so you do not need to worry about renewing your certification. You are investing in yourself and your career, so it is important to have an idea about what you want your career to look like in the future before committing to the course. Keep in mind that you will have your own personal expenses to contend with, especially if you need accommodations. To my knowledge, there are no scholarships for the course. However, the part-time course is less expensive than the full-time course, so that should be taken into account as you decide what is best for you. If you are still contemplating whether or not to take the course, and expense is a serious factor, consider a different course like TEFL (see Other Courses). This course is perhaps the cheapest out of all the ESL teaching courses and if offered more regularly than the CELTA. Remember, this is an investment in yourself and your future; you are worth it!

6. CHOOSING WHERE TO TAKE YOUR COURSE

Once you have decided to take the course, where can you actually go to complete it? Look to ESL schools in your area. There were two main English teaching schools in my area, and I debated which school would work best for me. I ultimately choose a chain ESL school in the hopes of forming a bond with that school and having more job opportunities in the future. Chances are, they offer the course a few times each year. If you find a few different schools, determine which is most convenient for you: is it close to home, do they offer accommodations if needed? The CELTA is also offered as an online course, if commuting each day is not a good option for you. More and more courses are being held online since COVID, and this offers you the chance to practice teaching online. The downside is you do not receive in-person teaching experience, which takes a vastly different approach than online teaching. Since the course is only offered a few times a year, be sure to make that schedule work for you. You do not want to make the decision to take the course and have to wait months before starting. Another thing to think about it, can I apply for a position at this school once I have completed the course? Look at all your options and research the different places that the course is available. On the Cambridge English website (see Other Tips), there is a handy course locater that tells you all the schools in your area that offer the course. If teaching in an ESL school is your goal, carefully consider what school is best for you. If you want to teach online, perhaps the online course is preferable.

7. LOCATION IS KEY

When choosing the right place to take your course, it is especially important to choose a location close to your home. For my course, the school offered convenient hotel accommodations less than 5 minutes away, which was a Godsend. Some of my peers lived over an hour away from the school and had to contend with public transport and traffic, sometimes waking up at 5:30am to get to class on time. I was lucky enough to be able to roll out of bed, grab my pre-packed lunched and enjoy the five-minute walk to class. This is a real help, especially as you will need extra time in the morning to print out material for your classes and get situated for the day. You do not want to contend with rush hour traffic, either before or after class. This will greatly cut into your valuable time, and let's face it— who wants to be stuck in traffic after a long day? If you decide to take the online course, location is a breeze but remember to make yourself a quiet space to conduct lessons and participate in the tutorials. For you parents out there who might prefer the online approach, make sure to stress that you will be unavailable during class time. Since the pandemic began, most people have become accustom to online work and already have measures in place to focus your time on work. This will be no different.

8. CELTA AND COVID-19

A week into my CELTA course, COVID-19 struck. Everyone was frantic, wondering if the course would continue and how we would manage a three-week course online. The organization and course teachers decided that the course would be extended and held online. The normally three-week program stretched into two months, with classes held online every day. Our lessons and tutorials utilized Zoom, which is what I use to conduct my lessons now. Zoom has plenty of helpful tools like screensharing, breakout rooms to separate groups for exercises, and that oh so handy mute button. We quickly learned how to teach using Zoom, utilizing break out rooms, screen sharing and dealing with technical problems. While we were unable to teach in-person, the extended course and mandatory lockdown allowed my CELTA group to experience on-line teaching and we had more time to complete assignments. This was a double-edged sword: on one hand, we had the ability to work from the comfort of our own home and the course allowed for additional time to complete the allotted work, teaching online is a very different animal than teaching in-person. Students become tired more easily, especially staring at the computer screen for three hours. You have to contend with technical issues, background noise and students who turn off their cameras mid-class.

9. PERSONAL LIFE ON PAUSE

Be prepared to put your personal life on pause. Forget about date nights, dinner with friends, holidays, even weekly exercise classes. You simply will not have enough time! The CELTA course will be your total focus, and because of the intensity of the workload, any spare time you have will be spent on much needed Rest and Relaxation. Make sure to tell your family and friends that you will be MIA for the duration of the course and put plans on hold. CELTA will become your focus for the duration of the course, and you need to manage your time well. While you need to have time for yourself and give yourself a break, think of each night like a school night—tomorrow, I need to be bright-eyed, prepared, enthusiastic, and ready for the long day ahead. So, no barhopping, even on the weekends. Weekends will be spent catching up on work, spending time with family, and doing that laundry you have been avoiding all week.

10. FORGET ABOUT THAT DIET

During my CELTA, the desire to lose 10 pounds quickly vanished. Ramen noodles, instant soups and sandwiches punctuated with the odd salad or steamed vegetable became the norm. I recommend meal preps on weekends; spend a few hours making the meals for the week. This way, you are ensured a healthy meal quickly and with little effort. There are so many useful videos out there for meal-prep ideas, so stock up on the weekend and enjoy that time in the kitchen. If cooking isn't your thing, make sure to buy some healthy, already cooked meals. You will need your energy for the CELTA. Treat yourself occasionally, and do not feel bad if the Chinese restaurant nearby starts to know your go-to order. Also, offer yourself some variety! Ham and cheese sandwiches for lunch every day gets pretty boring after a week. You will break for lunch every day for an hour, right after your teaching lesson and before your own learning begins. However, you will also be expected to document what has happened during the class and your own evaluation of your lesson. So, having a meal ready to pop in the microwave as you type away is always a bonus.

11. PRE-TASKS

After you have been accepted into the CELTA course, the work begins. Your first assignment will be due before you even enter the classroom. You will have to respond to 50 tasks that center around specific grammar points, pronunciation, teaching etiquette and lesson planning. Many of the terms and ideas will be known to you already, regardless of your experience level as a teacher. However, the pre-task is a great way to freshen up on the topics necessary to teach English to second language learners, like phonology, auxiliary verbs, sentence structure and learning context. The pre-task also lets you begin to focus on what sort of students you will be teaching in the course. All students are adult learners, with a different set of learning skills. You will begin to think about what kind of students you will have and how to mold your classes to fit this unique kind of student body. The pre-task is a great introduction to the course, as it will highlight many of the topics you will be studying over the route of the program and will put you in the learning mind space. Make sure to complete and send in prior to the course; you do not want to be the only person without their pre-task completed!

12. PREPARING FOR THE COURSE

Beside the logistics of where and when you will take the course, it is important to review your English fundamentals before-hand, focusing on what you know you struggle with. Personally, I abhor tenses with a passion, so I studied up on grammar tenses before my course. Use the pre-task to study. There is so much valuable information in the pre-task that will help you prepare. Picture it as an at home test, and write down what topics you struggle with, and what information to review later. Also, there is a plethora of different website you can find that can help you prepare for the small details of the course, like what exercises second language learners favor and how to present relevant material. You might be asked to purchase relevant books about teaching, but often times they will be made available to you after your course begins. It is not necessary to read these books before the start of the class, but if you like to get ahead, try to find free PDFs online to save on expenses or ask to borrow them from your ESL school's library. These books are written by experienced ESL teachers, and you will be asked to use quotes from them for your assignments.

13. NECESSARY TECH

Technical failures are a part of life, in and out of the classroom. Problems with audio, slideshow presentations and Wi-Fi immediately send a rush of nerves through you, especially during a lesson. Always be prepared for technical failures and (I cannot stress this enough) always backup your lessons and lesson plans. Have a USB handy; keeping all your files in one place and being able to immediately find the materials you need will save you time and stress. Be sure to have a secure Wi-Fi connection and a trusty computer. The last thing you need is to lose hours' worth of work because of technical difficulties. If your course is being held online, try to purchase a headset and microphone. You want to be as clear as possible, so your students and peers can hear you during class and tutorials. If you plan to teach online in the future, a working headset is a must.

14. THE NIGHT BEFORE

I could not fall asleep the night before my CELTA course started. So nervous to see what the day had in store, I tossed and turned in my hotel bed, battling with myself; was this a bad idea, what if I fail, what did I get myself into! Even though I knew I had a strong grasp of English, it had been years since I had been in the classroom. Those nervous thoughts are perfectly normal, so do not second guess yourself! Try to be as calm as possible and get a good night's sleep. Otherwise, you will spend your first day holding back yawns and rubbing puffy eyes, like I did. You will quickly fall into a routine and after the first week of the course, you will become accustom to the rigors of the course and develop your own ways of handing the stress. The night before your course begins, prepare what you will need for the day like a notebook, pens, computer, lunch, and breakfast. Even pick out the clothes you will wear. That way, all you have to is roll out of bed, pick up and go.

15. FIRST DAY JITTERS

Whether you are starting a new school, new job, or meeting coworkers for the first time, nervousness and doubt are bound to seep into you mind. The opening day of your CELTA will be about conquering those first day jitters and preparing yourself for your first lesson. Normally, you do not see your students until the 2nd or 3rd day of classes, so the first few days are about connecting with your fellow CELTA teachers; everyone awkwardly smiling at each other, breaking the ice, and comparing notes about teaching experiences. Your instructors will do warmup exercises with you, similar to the ones you will do with your own students during the first days of class. By the time you break for lunch, you will be chatting like old friends. These bonds will save you during your CELTA course and drastically help you deal with the stress and workload over the next few weeks. As they day goes by, your nervousness will dissipate as the mystery of the course wears away and you feel more comfortable in conquering what is expected of you.

16. WORKING TOGETHER: MEET YOUR PEERS

Usually, a maximum of 12 potential teachers are accepted during an in-person, full time CELTA course. Meeting your colleagues for the first time is always a bit nerve-wracking, but these people will quickly become your friends and confidants. After the initial awkwardness of a first-time meeting, you will come to rely on the other teachers in your course, whether it be help with a class or lesson, clarifying an assignment, or simply commiserating about how little sleep you are getting or how much work you have left to do. Learn to rely on your peers. Over the intensive course, you will need their help and support. Your fellow trainees will all have different teaching experiences: some might have been teaching for years while for others it will be the first time in a real ESL classroom. Experienced trainees can offer you a great deal of support and extend important tips about classroom etiquette and teaching strategies. When my course was completed, the trainees compiled all their lesson plans and shared them to each other for future use. There will certainly be people you do not connect with, but overall, your peers will be compassionate and willing to help you. Afterall, you are all in the same boat, rowing towards the same goal and trying to overcome the same turbulent seas.

17. MEET YOUR INSTRUCTORS

If you are lucky, like I was, you will have some amazing instructors. Their job is to monitor your teaching, point out where you excel and where you need to improve. They will guide you through the ins and outs of teaching. They will also give tutorials on teaching skills and grammar points. They grade your assignments, and their input will determine your overall success in the course. Instructors will be highly lauded and are past CELTA candidates themselves, so they know what you are going through. My instructors were amazing teachers and very understanding. During your teaching practice, your group will be run by one of these two candidates and they will guide you through your lessons, distributing material, assigning work. and making sure that you complete all the necessary milestones to pass the course. When you switch classrooms to teach a new proficiency level, you will be paired with the other instructor. Instructors are there to point out your attributes and provide critiques in order to improve your teaching skills. They will motivate to keep going even when it seemed impossible to continue and their support will stick with you for years to come.

18. TRUSTING YOUR INSTRUCTORS

In order to excel at the course, you must have faith and trust in your instructors. Most CELTA courses are run by impeccable and brilliant instructors whose only goal is to see you improve and pass the course. These instructors are teaching legends, who have been in the business for years and have seen numerous students pass through their doors. They have all been in your shoes, having passed the CELTA and the more intensive DELTA course for teaching instructors. Besides from being extremely intelligent and knowledgeable about the fundamentals of teaching, they will often help soothe those moments of general panic, when you doubt yourself and your abilities. The instructor that had a lasting impression on me was Brigid; a sharply intelligent woman, Brigid was always there to offer gentle support and guidance, along with a quick-witted zinger or two. All my fellow CELTA trainees gushed about how understanding and helpful she was during the course. Utilize your instructor's their knowledge and experience to learn how you can improve your own teaching. They will be a valuable asset during your CELTA journey.

19. MEET YOUR STUDENTS

When you walk into your first practical teaching lesson, around 15 shiny and bright faces will turn to you, just as apprehensive as you are. These students are not paying for the class— CELTA course instructors will gather students who are interested in a free English language course taught by budding teachers. Students will be separated depending on their understanding of the language into intermediate and pre-intermediate classes and will come from different countries from around the world. My course was predominately students from South America, many of them older than I was. At first, the fact that I was younger than my students took me for a loop. Would I garner the same respect and attention as my older peers? But as you step up to start your first lesson, you will realize that you have something valuable to share with students. ESL students are there to learn and are motivated to do well because they want to reach their goals. Some students will get bored and stop showing up, but the students that really want to learn will stick around and engage with you and other students. I found that my age was actually a boon, and students felt more comfortable with me and viewed me as a peer, albeit one that assigned them the homework at the end of the day. Enjoy getting to know your students and use teaching practice as just that— practice.

20. BREAKING THE ICE

Your first class with your new students will be very relaxed as you start to break the ice and get to know your students. Start with simple games to get the ball rolling. During my CELTA course, we played a game where we threw a ball back and forth, introduced ourselves, our favorite things to do, where we come from and why we were there. This helps relax the students and will relax you too. Even if students feel like this is a simple game without any real learning or practice to be had, remember that everyone is getting to know each other— not just you and your students, but the students interacting with other ESL learners. These warm-up games also allow students to practice vital skills that will prepare them for the more intricate lessons. Any activity that has students interacting, discussing and communicating with each other is a positive activity. Warm-ups and icebreakers will be used for every class to introduce the topics and get students speaking and thinking about the subjects they will be learning. It also provides some breathing room as they transition from one type of lesson to another.

21. CULTURE SHOCK

The wonderful thing about ESL students is that they come from around the world and have a different set of experiences. Your students will have encountered many of the same situations you have, though you might feel as if you come from vastly different lifestyles. We had students from Spain, Brazil, Russia, Nepal, and China, each with their own understanding and experience with English. As teachers, we need to respect and understand these differences. Most students are extremely respectful. Our Nepalese students would refer to us as "Miss/Mr. Teacher", while some of our Spanish students were more comfortable calling us by our first name. Be aware of the backgrounds of your students and always be respectful and courteous. Throughout your own learning tutorials about the fundamentals of teaching English to second language learners, you will discover the different ways ESL students process information and how culture influences each student. Keep in mind that words and situations you understand might not apply to other cultures. For example, I was conducting a lesson with three of my Chinese students, trying to elicit the word 'oven' (we were discussing different jobs people have and the tools they use). I was amazed to discover that the Chinese do not really use ovens and this piece of vocabulary was not something they had encountered before. Many ESL students rely on English television as the basis of their language knowledge, so they may be more accustom to slang and informal conversation. Keep culture in mind as you plan your lessons. You will get used to these differences as the weeks progress.

22. MOTIVES FOR LEARNING

Unlike middle school, high school and university students, most ESL students have decided on their own to improve their English; they are not pushed by their parents to learn, but instead are motivating themselves to practice. ESL students might want to improve their English for career opportunities, travel plans, or to build relationships. Each student has a motive for learning, and this means their targets and desires are different from the everyday student. One of my biggest motivations for teaching was that English is the most widely spoken language in the world and is now a necessary skill to have, either for work, travel or basic interaction. My belief is that something as simple as a conversation should not be the reason a qualified individual gets passed over for a job or important experience. Some student's goals are to excel in the business world, or to be able to write a strong resume to better their opportunities. These motives will drive students to succeed, and you will find that they work harder in the classroom than native English speakers. They have set objectives in mind and it is you job to help them realize those goals. However, be sure to assert yourself and have confidence in you lesson plan. I had a student who wanted to focus on pronunciation. 5 minutes into the class, he stopped me and wanted to dictate what we would cover in the lesson. Older students might feel like they have a better idea of their objectives than you do, which might be true; however, you have the knowledge and experience to know what should be taught and how. Stand by your lessons and do not allow bossy students to shake your confidence.

23. LET THE STUDENTS BE THE TEACHERS

The key to ESL and teaching in general is allowing students to teach and learn from each other. Never explain an answer to a given question. Instead, pose the question to the class: "What do you think the answer is?". A student that knows the answer can explain for you, lowering the amount of time you speak in the class (see What is TTT). This way, conversation flows, and students will feel more connected and confident with their peers, facilitating and motivating free speech practice. Each student has their own basis of knowledge; utilize this to your advantage and let the class fill in the blanks for each other. ESL students are like sponges— the soak up the most minute details and practicing with other ESL students teaches them informal conversation, which is important in day-to-day life. A student might know a particular saying or idiom and teach it to their classmates. However, if we notice a mistake during group discussions, we must be sure to correct it as to not foster false information. Students can also teach you what topics they are concerned with and what learning techniques they thrive on.

24. THE DO'S AND DO NOT'S OF TEACHING

It important to monitor our language to fit the proficiency level of the classroom. Students might not know the meaning of certain words and can be too nervous to ask for clarification. Temper your language to fit proficiency levels; a pre-intermediate class will have less of a 'mental lexicon' than an intermediate class, and you must be aware of the language you use. Similarly, speak slowly and calmly to ensure that students will catch every part of the lesson. Most importantly, become comfortable with silence, and do not feel pressured to fill the room with conversation or lecturing. Give students time to process and consider questions. Stray away from discussing religion, politics, and family issues. We want to simulate neutrality and take into account that we do not know the cultural differences of every background. Students might try to tempt you into straying from lessons to talk about these issues, but do not take the bait. It can lead to sticky situations.

25. NOT THE WORST TEACHER IN THE WORLD

We all remember that one teacher that made a lasting impression on us. We also remember, perhaps even more vividly, the worst teacher we ever had. Both examples are important for us to grow as teachers. We learn what we should do, how to inspire students, and what things to stray away from. In your most vulnerable moments, remember that you are certainly not the worst teacher in the world and even if you leave a class feeling as if you did not accomplish what you wanted, your next class is an opportunity to do better. Our perceptions of ourselves, in and out of the classroom, are often not as harsh or terrible as we think they are. I remember leaving a lesson feeling as if I totally blew the lesson.

As I relayed these fears to my peers and instructors, they assured me that I did not do as bad as I thought I did. As teachers, we learn in our classes just as much as the students do. It is all part of the journey. Always remember that you are growing as a teacher with each lesson and the mistakes you make in one class do not have to follow you to the next one. As long as you are engaging, explanative and encouraging, your lesson will not be a total failure. And even if you completely miss the mark, know that you will do better in the next lesson.

26. FEEDBACK

During the course, the potential teachers are separated into two groups for teaching practice: one group for intermediate students, and one for pre-intermediate students. Half-way through the course, groups switch classes as to allow teachers to practice different proficiency levels. Different proficiency levels require a new approach to your lesson plan and teaching style and your instructors will guide you on the dos and don'ts of the lesson structure. Your teaching group will work together to plan lessons, so each part of the lesson flows smoothly during the class. While your peers teach, you will be taking notes on their teaching styles, what they are doing right and, more importantly, what they are doing wrong. At the end of the lesson, you share with your peers and give them a general idea of what you found to be working and what was not as successful. Critiques should always be constructive and detailed, not a simple 'good/bad'; provide examples of exact moments in the lesson that were positive or negative. Besides giving feedback, you will receive your own from your peers and instructors and learn what you can improve and where you excel. Take feedback into account, because observers will notice things in the lesson that you might not.

27. TP (TEACHING PRACTICE) PREP

During teaching practice, you will conduct a section of the lesson for each class. One section might focus on grammar, another on pronunciation or speaking practice. For each class, you will be expected to prepare a lesson plan that details your objectives, what issues you might encounter, and a step-by-step break down of each part of the lesson.

Lesson plans are all similarly formatted, and you are given a handy template to use for each lesson. These lesson plans are very important, and you will use them as a guide for each lesson. If you ever get stuck during a lesson, just look down at you TP plan to center yourself and refocus. You will be evaluated on each lesson by your instructors, who will point out strengths and weaknesses in your lesson plan. This guidance should be used for each of your lessons, to show that you have understood the criticism and learned from it. You will also be expected to write a post-lesson self-evaluation where you answer questions about your own actions in the classroom. You will have to determine if the lesson was below standard, standard, or above standard. Be honest in your evaluations and note what changes you would make if you had to teach the material again.

28. MONITORING STUDENTS DURING OBSERVATION

While your peers are teaching you will be asked to monitor the students in your class: who is falling asleep, who is likely to volunteer, and what students are talking more about their personal lives then the assignment. We try to separate students who speak the same language, as they tend to fall into their native speech instead of practicing English. Take note of students and focus on a few that interest you. Notice where they excel and where they flounder. This will help during the Student Assignment, where you must analysis a particular student and their trouble points. You will also be given an observation booklet that will guide you through your observations in the classroom. Write down specific interactions and responses and note down the errors a particular student has made, verbatim. In addition to observing your students, you also need to observe your fellow teachers. Are the students engaged, is the teacher driving the lesson or are students participating actively? What is the teacher doing correctly and how are students responding to it? What is the teacher doing wrong or what can the teacher improve? These observations will be imperative during feedback and giving specific criticism can help everyone in the class learn.

29. MONITORING STUDENTS DURING YOUR LESSONS

We must monitor our students during class exercises and discussions by traveling around the classroom and speaking to individual students and groups during activities. Do not hover over students, because this could make them nervous. Instead, get down to their level and ask them to tell you a bit about what they are discussing. You can answer questions, and clarify that students are doing the assignment correctly. When we walk around the classroom during activities, it focuses students and signals that you are engaged in all areas of the lesson, including free practice and exercises. It is also a great time to learn more about your students and their strengths and weaknesses. Monitoring students during your lessons will also help you on your assignments (see 1st Assignment: Focus on the Learner). When you have chosen a student for this assignment, pay close attention to them as you monitor the classroom.

Are they actively engaging with other students during group discussions? What are their strengths when paired with different students? What are their weaknesses. We do not want to keep all our attention on one student, but we do want to keep an eye out for these issues for our assignment. There also might be stronger students that you will want to rely on if the class gets stuck on a problem. Use them when you need, but also try to include the entire class and open the discussion up to new students who might be too nervous to speak.

30. LESSON TYPES

To complete your CELTA, you need to teach a grammar, listening, reading, and writing class. Candidates will take turns teaching different topics and you will approach each topic differently. For example, grammar classes demand that you analyze your grammar point. Listening classes will require some technical skills and audio recordings, provided to you by the instructors. Reading classes will utilize material that must be printed before class and demands a bit of quiet time in the classroom while students digest the information. It is extremely helpful to watch your peers teach these different points and use their skills to help with your own approach to the lessons. What activities can you use to pair students together? What material is better suited for individual work or group discussion? We want to change up the practice and give students a mixture of paired, individual and group work. This way, students can learn from and practice with each other, while also allowing their own skills to flourish. Your instructors will assign worksheet pages from a specific ESL practice book, probably published by Cambridge University, so do not worry about scouring the web for exercises.

31. LESSON PLANNING

Lesson planning is a huge part of the CELTA course. You are expected to complete a lesson plan for each lesson you give, marking down the goals, anticipated problems, and solutions, and break down the time limit for each activity. You will be given resources to follow and exercises to draw from but will be expected to use your own skills to create lead-ins to the lesson. While we want to be organic in the classroom, and not simply read from a template, it is important to have a structure to your lesson. You will receive feedback about your lesson plans from instructors and will be graded based on the strength of your lesson. You will also have to keep the time limit in mind. Each of your lessons will be 45 minutes and your plans will have to break down how long you spend on an exercise. Your lesson plan should include your introduction to the material, the different activities students will perform and back-up exercises.

32. PRE-TEACH

For each lesson, you must determine if there are vocabulary words or situations that need to be explained for students to understand the lesson as a whole. We can use pictures and CCQs to extract the meaning of the word or situation for students and we must be sure to cover the meaning, form and pronunciation for all pre-teaching. Remember not to explain but elicit a response from students and let students teach each other by sharing their knowledge of a topic. Not every lesson will demand that you pre-teach something, but it will be up to you to put yourself in your student's shoes and determine what words, phrases or situations need to be explained. The pre-teach section of your class should not be longer than 10 minutes. You want to spend a majority of the lesson diving into the material, and which context is important, practice and production are our goals.

33. TARGET LANGUAGE

Your instructors will talk a great deal about target language. Target language is the specific language points or practice that the lesson focuses on. Is there a particular word or grammar point you want your students to practice? Our activities will center around these language points and our aim is to present the target language in context, so students can relate this focus to real life situations, garnering a connection with the language and associations with their actual experiences. We want students to incorporate the target language into their responses during the class and ensure that they are using it correctly. It might be difficult to image how a grammar point can become relatable to students, but through relevant activities, students can practice using different verbs, prepositions and tenses, preparing them for real life situations.

34. AUTHENTIC MATERIAL

Authentic material is a vital part of our lessons because it motivates students and instills connections between the target language and real life. We want to meet the interest of our students and relate topics that they are excited about. Authentic material can be anything from news articles, supermarket brochures, menus, ads, and advice columns. It is fun to incorporate these materials in your lessons, especially to allow students to practice speaking about a topic they have knowledge about. I always found authentic material to be a fun way to mix the target language with real life experience and connect the lesson with information students already know. It facilitates conversation, exposes students to real life issues, and gives them a reason to learn and engage. Your instructors will supply you with these exercises for your classes, but you will have to find your own material in order to complete one of your assignments (see 3rd Assignment: Language Related Task).

35. PHONICS

A big part of ESL teaching is phonics and pronunciation, so it is no wonder that special attention is put on mastering this. Pronunciation can drastically affect communication between yourself and your students. You will be asked to review the phonetic alphabet and learn about the specific issues that different cultures have with pronunciation. A great book that you will be introduced to is <u>Learner English: A Teacher's Guide to Interference and Other Problems</u>, by Swan and Smith, which goes in-depth about the pronunciation issues each culture has. This will be particularly important later in the course, when you are asked to single out a student and discuss their strengths and weaknesses. Regarding the phonetic alphabet, which isolated different sounds that are represented by their own unique symbol, you do not need to memorize this or incorporate the exact symbols into your lessons. Students do not need to know these specifics to master the language, but they do need to be able to pronounce words clearly. Pronunciation is an important part of communication, so make sure to incorporate this into your lessons.

36. GRAMMAR ANALYSIS

I detest tenses with a passion, but CELTA forced me to overcome my distaste for explaining them to students. Grammar analysis is a necessary evil when teaching ESL students and native speaking teachers who have not had a grammar lesson since middle school will find this equally frustrating. During grammar analysis, you must break down a sentence like it is a mathematical equation: a subject + verb in past tense + verb in progressive tense +preposition+ object = a complex sentence. Grammar analysis will be required when teaching a grammar lesson and during the Language Related Assignment. I relied on my peers to help me discern how to articulate form to students and slowly began to get better at teaching tenses. You will be given a template in which to follow, and since it is mandatory to have a grammar lesson, you want to be prepared to explain the grammar point to students and answer any questions they might have.

37. WHAT IS TTT

Now, let's talk about the CELTA acronyms. The CELTA course loves acronyms and there are numerous teaching points highlighted in this way. First is TTT or Teacher Talk Time— who speaks the most in the class? In our own learning experiences, whether in middle school, high school or university, teachers tend to lecture about the given subject and students tend to listen. When teaching ESL, it is imperative for the students to do most of the speaking. This way, they can practice their speaking and listening with other students. Your instructors will focus on this point and tell you to monitor your TTT. Pose questions that will elicit responses from the students and have students read instructions. During free practice, you can separate students into groups to discuss the topic or target language; be sure to monitor the groups to ensure they are speaking about activity and not something else. ESL students, despite their differences, are able to converse quite well with each other, so make sure to utilize this to limit your TTT.

38. WHAT IS PPP

PPP, or Presentation, Practice and Production, are the life's blood of teaching ESL students. This is all about how the students can digest the target language, use exercises to build vital skills, and reproduce the target language organically. First, we must PRESENT the material in context for the student, so students can relate what we are teaching to real life. This could be through pictures, authentic materials like blogs or pre-teaching vocabulary. Next, students PRACTICE together, learning from each other and can respond to the material in a controlled way, through specific exercises. These exercises can center around reading, writing, speaking and listening, tied together with group discussion. Your exercises will be taken directly from ESL practice books, so do not worry about searching the web for exercises. Lastly, and most important, students must PRODUCE on their own, mainly through discussion. This free practice helps students become comfortable with the material and accustom to specific grammar or reading points. Free practice will be based on what specific lesson type you are teaching that week (reading, writing, speaking, grammar). When forming your lesson plans, PPP should be at the forefront of your mind, with organic production of target language being the main focus.

39. WHAT IS MFP

MFP will be imperative to determine if students really understand what you are teaching them. For example: You pose a sentence to students— "It is **raining cats and dogs**"— and elicit what the MEANING of the bolded words are, using gestures and CCQ's (concept check questions) to make sure students understand the meaning of the sentence. Meaning always comes first and it is imperative that you practice conveying meaning in a relatable way. Use what students already know and general information that the class can connect to. Next is FORM— what are the parts of speech in the sentence? Form mainly covered grammar, the breakdown of each word in the sentence. In the example sentence, for instance, you can take the word "raining" and elicit the tense of the word, asking CCQs to clarify if the action takes place in the past, present of future. Last is PRONUNCIATION. Drill words through repetition, isolate syllables and ensure that students are pronouncing the language correctly.

We can use different techniques to articulate this, like counting syllables on our fingers or breaking down the word by the different sounds that we produce. Regardless of the type of lesson you are teaching, MFP will be a vital part of your CELTA experience and your overall success in the course.

40. WHAT ARE CCQS

CCQ's, or Concept Check Questions, help the teacher ensure that students understand what you have just taught them. ESL students tend to be on the shy side—whether because of their pronunciation or uncertainty, students might nod and say yes if you simply ask, "Do you understand?" or will not pose questions even if you ask, "Do you have any questions?". Instead, we use CCQ's to connect unknown words with known words and allow students to make connections and understand on their own. We can ask "is it this/is it that" and elicit yes/no responses to make sure that students understand the topic. CCQs are extremely important because want to stimulate conversation, articulate meaning, form and pronunciation, while making sure that students will be able to use the language point correctly. You will learn about CCQs during your tutorials with instructors, so be sure to ask questions when you are confused and observe your peers as they teach to get into the habit of asking these kinds of questions.

41. WHAT ARE ICQS

Like CCQ's, ICQ's, or Instruction Check Questions, are used to make sure students understand the instructions you give them. You do not want time for an exercise to go by and realize that students were not sure what exactly you wanted them to do. ICQ's ask students to repeat instructions step by step. We can ask "What are we doing first?", "Are we working together or by ourselves" or "Should we do this/that?". This way, we are certain that students understand what tasks we are asking them to complete. I found ICQs easier to master than CCQs, but your instructors will drill these details and make sure that you are comfortable using them. Your instructors will also want to make sure that you are using both ICQs and CCQs in class, so be sure to incorporate them into your lesson plan. As the weeks progress, you will become accustom to using these tools in the classroom and as your experience grows, you will be using ICQs and CCQs like a natural.

42. TIME MANAGEMENT: IN THE CLASSROOM

When I had my very first teaching practice, I was amazed by how quickly 45 minutes pass. I remember looking at the clock, realizing I still had 10 minutes left and that I was almost done with the exercises I prepared. That is why having a back-up exercise is so important. If you find yourself with extra time, be sure to have a task for students to complete in case you have gone through the material too quickly. Since each teaching practice must be 45 minutes long, to complete the allotted number of teaching hours, you do not want to finish your class early and have nothing for students to do. Always have a back-up! Back-ups should be fun, free-practice activities and games to stimulate participation and have students practice their speaking. Make sure your back-ups are centered or related to the subject matter you are teaching, perhaps involving the target language or connected talking points. You can even take note of the lesson directly following yours and confer with that teacher to settle on a back-up that works for both of you.

43. 1ST ASSIGNMENT: FOCUS ON THE LEARNER

Now, let's talk about the assignments. Probably my favorite assignment out of the four tasks needed to pass the CELTA course was Focus on the Learner. This assignment instructs you to focus on one student in your class, analyze their strengths and weakness and give suggestions on how that student can improve their English. Start thinking about which student you want to choose early in the course. You will interview the student and use your own observations to demonstrate their trouble-points. You will also need to quote examples of your student's particular weak spots, whether it be pronunciation, grammar, reading or writing. Use the Swan and Smith book previously mentioned to isolate what problems your student and use what you have learned in the class to recommend activities that the student can use to improve. This book is extremely valuable, as it goes into detail about the specific language problems each culture faces, particularly pronunciation issues. Since your classes will also be recorded by your instructors, use the audio for your lessons to isolate the issues your student faces.

44. 2ND ASSIGNMENT: LANGUAGE RELATED TASK

This was the task that I struggled with the most, even though it seems pretty straightforward. Unlike the other assignments, which are all in essay format, you are given a marker sentence to analyze and explain how you would teach that language point. You must break down the sentence; what is the MFP for the target language, how you would relate this language to real life (building context), and what are the anticipated problems and solutions. If you are also pre-teaching vocabulary, you must also show how you would convey and check the meaning using CCQs and pictures. Your instructors will help you immensely by pointing out exactly what needs to be fixed to get a passing score. Use your fellow CELTA trainers to compare notes and ideas. Remember that you only have to pass three assignments out of four, so if you struggle with this task, it will not make or break your success in the course. You instructors are always there to answer questions; they can not give you exact answers but can help guide you to the right direction and will do the best they can to make sure you pass these assignments.

45. 3ᴿᴰ ASSIGNMENT: LANGUAGE SKILLS TASK

The Language Skills Task is a fun assignment where you get to practice your lesson planning. First, you must choose a piece of authentic material and explain why this text is relevant to students. I choose an article about the Olympics because every student will know at least something about the topic, which is important for connection and speaking practice. Next, you must break down each part of the lesson, from your introduction of context to pre-teaching vocabulary and exercises and activities that the class would complete. You will also need to use quotes from teaching books like <u>Learning Teaching: The Essential Guide to English Language Teaching</u> by Jim Scrivener to support your ideas for lesson activities. Like any academic essay, you will need these quotes as evidence to support your argument. Instead of searching through the many books that can be used for evidence, use the table of contents to focus on your specific point. It is not required to read all the books given to you. They are more like guides to help you navigate the classroom and elicit discussion from your students.

46. 4TH ASSIGNMENT: LESSONS FROM THE CLASSROOM

The last assignment is also a fun, essay-formatted task that focuses on you, and your journey as a teacher. You must write between 750- 1000 words and refer to feedback from the classroom and your self-evaluations. Like the Focus on the Learner assignment, you must comment on your strengths and weakness in the classroom and determine what kind of teacher you are: are you friendly and bubbly? Do you give plenty of encouragement? Do you use a more serious approach to your lessons? The feedback from peers and instructors will be instrumental for this task, so pay attention after teaching practice and write notes about your feedback. Write about the areas that you excel and the places you need to work on, and how you intend to do so. This assignment also asks you to talk about what you plan on doing after

CELTA and how you plan on improving your teaching experience, so have an idea about your future goals and how to achieve them. Instructors want to see that you are actively working on building you experience and continuing your teaching journey in a viable way.

47. BALANCING UNDER PRESSURE

Given the intensity of the course, you are bound to experience pressure and panic. You will be pulling plenty of all-nighters, putting together lesson plans, finishing assignments, and preparing for the next tutorial. Over the course of CELTA, you will definitely feel periods of doubt and question your decisions and abilities. Do not let your inner saboteur win! You got into the course for a reason, and often we feel like we did worse in a TP or assignment then we actually did. Additionally, we tend to compare ourselves to other teachers, without taking into account different experience levels and abilities. Like in life, there is no use comparing yourself to someone else. They might have strengths that you do not, but the reverse is also true. Instead of feeling bad for yourself, use observation time to gain experience

50 Things to Know

from other teachers in the class. If students can learn from other students, we can learn from our peers. Trust the feedback from your instructors and fellow teachers, and when you need to take a break, take one! Even if it is a 15-minute walk around your block, set aside time for yourself to relax. These mini breaks are important for your mental and physical health. Remember: if you are hungry, eat; if you are tired, take a nap; if you have been sitting down in front of your computer too long, go outside and run around your block. Listen to your body and give it what it needs.

48. TIME MANAGEMENT: AT HOME

Manage your time to make the most out of your CELTA experience. Most of your day will be spent in the classroom, conducting your lessons, and taking part in teaching tutorials, so your time is extremely valuable. The first thing I would do after leaving class for the day would be settling down in front of my computer with a cup of tea and a banana, reviewing what I learned that day and preparing for the coming lessons. Stay on top of your assignments and stick to deadlines to complete these tasks. Think to yourself what assignments are due soon and which ones can I put on the back burner for a few days? In a three-week intensive course, you will receive a new assignment each week to complete, in addition to your daily lessons. I recommend knocking your lesson plans out first, taking a small break to refuel, then start working on your assignment. You do not want to be scrambling the night before to complete important assignments or have an incomplete lesson plan. Since the lesson plans are all templated the same, you can build off the information you already have and save time. In my case, we received the material for our lessons either a day or two before the planned class, so unfortunately you can not complete all your lesson plans in one swoop. This is actually helpful, because the information is fresh in your mind, and you are focused on the material you are going to teach. Plan your time at home wisely; as tempting as it is to check up on emails, watch an episode of a show or catch up with friends, keep on top of your assignments and lesson plans or you will definitely fall behind, which is never a good thing with CELTA!

49. NOW YOU HAVE YOUR CELTA, WHAT NEXT?

You have finished your course, passed with flying colors, and are now out in the real world, a fresh newly certified teacher! What now? After my course, I immediately began finding ESL students on my own, using different networks to find potential clients, even Facebook. Since COVID has closed many language schools, it is important to start finding students on your own to keep practicing your teaching and build yourself as a business. Branding yourself as a Cambridge certified ESL teacher will open new doors and you should use the connections you have made during the course to get ahead. Unfortunately, most schools will not let you carry on with your CELTA students after the course as an issue of privacy protection. However, use the resources available at the ESL school; ask if you can teach a free English class or apply for a full or part time position. Whatever you decided to do, the most important thing is to continue teaching and gain experience. You do not want your teaching skills to become rusty after a long break from the classroom. You can start your own tutoring business if you have marketing skills or set up ads around your neighborhood for people who want to improve their English. When COVID regulations have lessened and travel becomes more regular, look into teaching schools around the world, particularly in China. I am always seeing ads on Facebook from Chinese ESL schools offering full and part time positions. If you have missed traveling and have a place in mind that's calling your name, look into ESL schools in that country or area and start planning your future.

50. OTHER COURSES

There are numerous ESL teaching courses you can take before or after your CELTA. Depending on where you are from, there are three additional courses that might interest you. First is TEFL, or Teaching English as a Foreign Language. This course is shorter than the CELTA in duration and ranges in intensity. The TEFL is cheaper but you are not required to complete a teaching practice, which does not add that extra classroom experience. TESOL, or Teaching of English to Speakers of Other Languages, is good for domestic teaching or if you plan on pursuing a Master's degrees in ESL. TESL, or Teaching English as a Second Language depends on your goals; do you want to teach in your native country or abroad? TESL is good to teach in a country where English is a first language. CELTA, of course, allows you to teach anywhere in the world and does not expire. You pass once, you are set! It all depends on what you want your career to look like and what opportunities you want available. For teachers who have passed their CELTA, another course is available to you: the DELTA. The DELTA or Diploma in Teaching English to Speakers of Other Languages is an advanced course for teachers with at least one year of teaching experience under their belt. This diploma is for educators who wish to take supervising roles, like instructing teacher training or head English departments in ESL schools. Your instructors in the CELTA course will have passed the DELTA, so if you are inspired by your teachers during the course and want to emulate their career paths, the DELTA is right for you.

OTHER HELPFUL RESOURCES:

There is a plethora of different sites that can help you prepare for your CELTA and beyond. Since there are so many ESL teaching sites and schools, it can be overwhelming to find the one that works for you. If teaching online is your goal, apply to as many online ESL schools as you can. Many of your applications will not be responded to, as online teaching has boomed over the last year, but it is better to try your luck than not apply at all. If your application is accepted, many schools will ask you to interview with them or send in an introduction video. They may even ask for a video of a mock lesson. Be sure to dress appropriately and have a neutral background. Brand yourself as a professional and serious teacher, but also show your personality and how you would act in the classroom. Have fun and embrace the chaos!

Off 2 Class

Off 2 Class is a great tool to use for finding students, answering questions, and collecting resources for your lessons. Their website and Facebook page offer conversations about lesson points and you can connect with other ESL teachers around the world.

https://www.off2class.com/

Cambridge English

Another useful website is Cambridge English. Here, you can find resources for students, teachers and organizations and explanations about language points. I use this site to clarify grammar questions and utilize their exercises in my lessons. You can also find ESL schools and other locations to take numerous ESL courses, including the CELTA.

https://www.cambridgeenglish.org/

FluentU

FluentU offers valuable videos about ESL lessons and is another great place to meet other ESL teachers. Their blog also discusses important issues that ESL students face and how we as teachers can combat those problems. Topics also include exercises for your lessons and websites that you can apply to as a teacher. This site is instrumental in helping you navigate the intricate world on online teaching.

https://www.fluentu.com/blog/educator-english/

READ OTHER 50 THINGS TO KNOW BOOKS

50 Things to Know About Coping With Stress: By A Mental Health Specialist by Kimberly L. Brownridge

50 Things to Know About Being a Zookeeper: Life of a Zookeeper by Stephanie Fowlie

50 Things to Know About Becoming a Doctor: The Journey from Medical School of the Medical Profession by Tong Liu MD

50 Things to Know About Knitting: Knit, Purl, Tricks & Shortcuts by Christina Fanelli

50 Things to Know

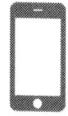

Stay up to date with new releases on Amazon:
https://amzn.to/2VPNGr7

CZYKPublishing.com

50 Things to Know

We'd love to hear what you think about our content! Please leave your honest review of this book on Amazon and Goodreads. We appreciate your positive and constructive feedback. Thank you.

Printed in Great Britain
by Amazon